the edge of the forest

Grant Caldwell

Grant Caldwell is a poet, novelist and academic. He has published poetry, fiction and articles in journals in Australia, Canada, China, Colombia, Germany, India, Ireland, Italy, Japan, New Zealand and U.S.A. His work has been translated into Bengali, Mandarin, Japanese, Spanish and Arabic. He has represented Australia at international poetry festivals in China, Colombia, New Zealand and Japan. He is a Senior Lecturer in the Creative Writing program at the University of Melbourne.

Acknowledgments

Many of these poems shave been published before in Grant Caldwell's books and the following journals and magazines:

Arena, Ampersand, Blast, Blue Dog, Blue Light Lounge, Chelsea Hotel (Germany), *Clouds Peak* (U.S.A.), *Ekleksographia* (Canada), *Famous Reporter, Germinal, Ginyu* (Japan), *Going Down Swinging, Haiku Harvest* (U.S.A.), *Heat, Meanjin, mod_piece, Moving Galleries, Newcastle Poetry Prize Anthology* (2007), *Off the Page, Off the Record, Otis Rush, Poetry Ireland Review, P76, Saltlick, Scarp, Space New Writing, Spit* (U.S.A), *Strange Shapes, The Age, The Best Australian Poems 2008, The Best Australian Poetry 2007, The Sydney Review, Thylazine, Tokyo Poetry Festival Anthology 2008* (Japan), *Towards the Impossible – Anthology of 2005 Wellington International Poetry Festival, Unusual Work, Verso, World Haiku Anthology* 2007/08/09/10 (Japan), *Yapanchitra – International Poetry Issue* (India), *Your Friendly Fascist.*

Contents

hardly able to focus

the monkey is meditating
on the pointlessness of squares
the visitors take snapshots of their expectations
the monkey articulates form and emptiness
the visitors are enthralled at the sounds
their laughter like the call of birds
echoes around the cage
the monkey mistakes it
for the phantoms of its tribe
it rushes after them among
the broken trees and rocks
the visitors are screaming with laughter
they point their cameras
hardly able to focus

sunday – the sun is out

the sun is out
the wind blowing
late afternoon
early summer
i walk to bronte beach
watch the waves
the surfers
the joggers the
power-walkers with their little coloured hand weights
the tight families picnicking in the park
with their children their dogs their eskies their
large checked blankets
taking paper plates boxes bottles refuse to the bins
one man slaps himself on the back to keep warm
i walk in the shallows
into the rock pools
    watching these tiny little flies
    racing frantically back and forth
    across the moss-covered rocks
    and the ultra-green seaweed
    wavering in the clear water
and walking back up the valley
negotiating the soccer volleyball baseball cricket games
into the quiet clear upper reaches of the park
a man
    sitting to one side
calls to me
can you help me up please mate? he says
eh? i say

can you help me up please mate? he says again
i can't get up
i haven't been drinking
            i just can't get up
so i help him
            he's heavy
            feels like he'll
            fall down again
you okay? I say
yes thank you thank you very much mate he says
you sure you're okay? I say
                        wondering what i'll do
                        if he says no
yes i'm fine thank you he says
well don't sit down again i say smiling
no he smiles back
no i won't
i walk further up the park and beyond
see lovers
            sitting on the grass
            or
            standing together
            about to hug
            by white fences
and when i get home
i open all the windows
lie on the floor
and fly away…

this morning
in the letterbox–
sunlight

a man passing
on the footpath–
followed by a plastic bag

a butterfly–
flies in and out
of the birdcage

in the trees
the sound of movement –
wind

across the sea

the sea comes
across itself
here it comes
across itself
see it coming
it comes and comes
across itself
it keeps coming
it never stops
here it comes
see it coming
across itself
it comes and comes
over and over
it keeps coming
across itself
over and over
see it coming
here it comes
look at it coming
it never stops
it keeps coming
look at it coming
over and over
across itself
see it coming
over and over
forever and ever
look at it coming

over and over
across itself
it keeps on coming
it never stops
see it coming
across itself
over and over
it never stops
it keeps coming
over and over
forever and ever
it never stops
it never stops
look at it
it never stops

the art of gambling

carnival of light

yellow on blue light
particles you hear
from the bubble you inhabit
a tick
like an insect
a sprinkler
throwing sound or water
into the light

the art of gambling

painting the lightest room you can find
always towards the window
you swallow yourself like a habit
the telescoped brain
breathe out breathe in
the lowest rock looks up
the beauty of a baby's smile
the way dogs talk
or trees
limitations give shape
the secret of every difference is direction
solitude in the crowd
fana or nirvana
to blow the mind away
slow as a universe

singing in the storm

it takes forever
to appreciate your limitations
the barrier of sky
shoots after a bushfire
green on death
the silence rings
the hatred of history
a sky of clouds
raining on faces like flowers

the unsaid hand

curling the long beach
the sea-breath gulls hang on
a woman walking the coast
carrying a man's heart she didn't ask for
but wanted all the same
the intangibility of emotion
knocks you like an elephant

the pleasure of habit
you find your measure of
in confusing spirals
the flux of wings
the bang
of miraculous aberrations

a blues song

this song is called
i've got the
downer
bummer
life's a joke and i'm the joker
down and out
hangdog
lonesome
broken hearted
self-pitying
good night nurse
they took away the tv
and the radio's on the blink
cockroach riddled
no goodies
can't afford to be sick
life was meant to be hard
    swimming upstream
    or standing cold and lonely on the brink
bronchitic claustrophobic paranoiac suicidal
tension-sprung insomniacal
eye-strained
down-at-heeled
holes in everything
and my teeth are rotting
men in uniforms scare me silly
hyped up
spaced put
slapped in

held under
it's all over
soaked thru
in between
freaked out
frazzled
even the tai chi won't help
or you
who wants to know
sick of pushing
things are crook in tallarook
all time low
even up's a down

BLOOOOOOOOOOOOZ!

on the mortal vanity of appearances

these were the excuses
like how time flies   hello
words as things and symbols
so important to be exact
encased in a kind of perusal
moments like balloons
fly the wall-less room

your body a lump
surveys the scene
a million things placed
without great reason
saying what it's not
the peripheral power of the eye

we're on the beach now
dusk
the sea seems loud
birds like phantoms
pecking at shadows

you know what i mean

for F.P.

he came around
to my darlinghurst rooms
and we had a joint
and talked about art and
bullshit
for a while
then he told me
his idea
for a performance
he was doing
at the basement
that coming saturday
he was going to get a live sheep
and slaughter it
in a bathtub
just cut its throat
and watch the blood
fill the bath.
what do you think? he said
he had this half-mad grin on his face.
the only problem is, he continued
suddenly serious,
i don't know if i'll be able
to get a sheep.

i changed the subject then
and pretty soon it got on to music

and he asked me
if i'd noticed
how the words of the latest men at work song
were really a message to him
warning him
that they were
out to get him
for what he knew.
knew about what? i asked.
i can't tell you, he said
but you know what i mean.

i looked at him.
yes, i said

i know what you mean
and it's true
i did
and

i

do

glass clouds

in salutation to your broken genius
no mirrors but
the windowed wall you
create and the light
breaks the glass clouds where
this morning's broken
genius lets go like a
flower a bee the latest gadget
everything contained in a thought
encompassing empty thrills
the grand illusion is bright today
how serious you are etcetera,
the definition of love is
where are you now and no
is a freedom we forget so much
regret and striving the broken
music of silence comes
quickly into the room
listening to your breathing

mundane avenues of compensation

the daily habits
you absently flatter yourself for
like recycling or being kind to insects

of course there are other games available
like fish or water
or guess who that is up in the tree

meanwhile
paying the rent
is a major achievement

and those moments you think
how pointless your last hour has been
nudge you like desire
into new depths of ontology

watching braveheart on tv

watching braveheart on tv
thousands of ants
come marching down the hall
and into the lounge
where they come to a halt.

they stretch back up the hallway out of sight.

the tv goes dead.
everything is silent.
we stare at each other across the burgundy carpet.
many of them are all holding spears or swords or axes
some have splashes of war paint on their faces.
the one at the front has a blue and red face.
it raises its sword and yells cross the room at me

YOU CAN TAKE OUR LIVES
BUT YOU'LL NEVER
TAKE
OUR FREEDOM!!!

and the thousands behind it
raise their arms and yell their assent
and they begin to charge

words in arc light

the truth is
everything is a lie
freedom is a word
with locks on it
and there's no key
to careful abandonment
the inuit have five words for snow
the aztecs have one for rain, hail and snow
the bark of trees
is pissed on by dogs
i read somewhere
arc lights in a sawmill
make the blade seem still

the lights are on

the irony of green rain
is not lost on you

the rank apocalypse
stalks the landscape

spreadable butter for your convenience
where would we be without

your depressive head
mocks you from its alcove

cars whizz both ways
the question remains

like a daytime tv show
where someone you're sure

is yourself in disguise
makes predictable jokes

laughed at by machines

three leaves
in the bird bowl –
passing clouds

silent tree –
the sky
moves you

at night this winter
tree shadow on a white wall –
where is the moon?

in the garden
late at night –
distant music

ozone but

with my hat
at the beach

dotted with death tans
i want to scream ozone but

i keep my shirt on

the sea throws up on the shore
and only the sky seems clean

and on the bus home
a lobster-red boardie
with zinc-green nose

says wow
look at those beautiful flowers
shit yair her friend agrees

while the bus driver
is making noises
like his steering wheel

need to speak

the little boy always has attention
but not from those he wants
he lives in the tree house of his dream
he imagined once was real
all the petty actions outside
the need to speak
squashed into otherness
where beyond knowing
the revelations are filmic
he is there all his life
the words and phrases come like surprising birds
they speak for him to the skyness
they are his interpreters his translators
he trusts in their faith (he has no choice
the trinkets of his effort
shine like flowers in the rain
he is forever seeking
the umbrella for his pain

the fat bread

in the park

the arrowfast tortoise

                                          shell

cat

                                          stalks

the fat bread

                                          bloated

pigeons

pecking the sun

                                          dry

grass

the neverending poem

At Stephen Hawking's
public lecture
about the universe
being enclosed in an immense bubble
an elderly woman interrupted him
declaring
'You're wrong young man:
the universe is sitting on the back of a turtle.'
'Ah yes, Hawking nodded,
'that's all very well but
what's the turtle standing on?'
and she replied:
'It's turtles
all
the
way
down!'

Sign in a shop window:
                    GIANT SALE

In Europe in 1990
the production of cars
is outstripping the birth rate

Newspaper headline:
HOLE IN HEART BOY
KILLED BY FALLING WINDOW

A newspaper report
of a suicide note
left by a man
who bashed an elderly woman to death
has two four-letter words
dotted out

Royal Society for the Blind billboard
                SOME PEOPLE
                CAN'T SEE THE FOREST
                OR THE TREES

some band names circa 1990
                    Gasoline Kisses
                    Exploding White Mice
                    Mutated Noddies
                    Lubricated Goat
                    Fresh Rectum
                    Hot God Vomit

The electric blue neon sign
above the Electricity Commission building
declares
            E CTRICITY
            COMMISSION
a week later
it just says
            COMMISSION
and another week later
            OMMISSION

Graffiti on the inside fence of a large
inner city demolition site
in huge white letters
reaching all the way around the vacant lot
AND THE ETERNAL SILENCE OF INFINITE SPACE
REMAINS AS INDIFFERENT TO OUR FATE AS EVER
A week later
the words have been painted over with white paint

C.E.M Joad
writing of A.N. Whitehead
in his Guide to Philosophy:
'That Whitehead's views are of first-rate
importance is almost universally agreed
but there is no sort of agreement
as to what they are.'

Sign in a shop window
                    MIDDLE CLASS
                    CABINET MAKER

TV reporter:
'In the USA every weekend
18,000 people shoot
water-based die pellets
at each other
in simulated war games.
One of the organisers said
From a corporate standpoint
it's a tremendous morale booster

some people say it only encourages
a war-mongering attitude
I say
it's just the opposite
it teaches people
a healthy respect
for weapons of war.

On a large cardboard box
in the back of a truck
        THIS BOX CONTAINS
        500 HOURS
        FREE TIME

Headline in the Daily Mirror
50 YEARS OF HEADLINES!

An article in the newspaper
under the title
BE KIND TO TOADS
'According to the RSPCA,
spraying cane toads
with chemicals or
bashing them with gold clubs
is cruel, unnecessary and illegal.
Just because they are ugly
and destructive pests
is no excuse for cruelty.
The RSPCA recommends
placing the toads in plastic bags
and freezing them to death.'

A man using a machine
to blow the leaves
off his driveway

Classified advertisement
in MONEY STOCKS & SHARES
    'if you can invest $2,000,000
    I can make you rich
    phone ....'

Newspaper article:
KRAY IN LONDON HOSPITAL
'Ronnie Kray
one of the notorious gangland twins
serving life in prison for murder
is in hospital after a suspected
heart attack.
The killer,
who at 59
smokes 100 cigarettes a day,
was in high security Broadmoor
special hospital after collapsing
while trying to strangle another prisoner
whose whistling got on his nerves.'

'Economics is the method
the aim is to change the human soul.'
                    Margaret Thatcher

the life of a pet dog

you give a dog a bone and
feeling good
you pat it on the head.
the next day it comes back
so you pat it on the head
and feeling good
you give it a bone.
the following day it returns
so you give it another bone
and pat it on the head
and give it some biscuits
and send it away.
the day after that it fails to come
but the following day it turns up
with its tail wagging and face smiling
so you give it a bone
and talk to it
and pat it on the head
feeling good.
it hangs around outside
and sleeps on the old chair in your yard.
so the next day it's around about
and you give it a bowl of water
and pat it on the head
calling it *boy*
and take it with you
when you go to the shops
feeling good
and you buy it some biscuits

which you've noticed it seems to like.
after a week or so
the dog is at your place
almost every day
and your friends say
you've got a dog
and you say
yes, i suppose i do
and tho you pretend otherwise
you're feeling good because of it.
another week goes by
and yes, you decide
you do have a dog.
so you stock up on tins of dog food
and buy it a flea-collar
and have it inside a few cold nights.
and after a few months
it's inside more than out
and it grows fatter
and seems to hang about
about the time you always feed it
and you don't like going away
without taking it with you
and tho it still makes you feel good
to pat it and talk to it
and watch it wag its tail
and smile
you don't feel as good as when you first had it.
so after a few years
although it seems quite happy
it has grown even fatter
its teeth have begun to rot
and a growth has appeared in its testes

and although you still feel okay
walking it down the street
and in the park
you don't feel that great about it anymore.
a few more years pass
and it gets another growth
now on its side
more noticeable
and the vet says its cancerous
but no it doesn't hurt him
and anyway his heart condition
and his nervous disorder
which make it unwise to try and remove it
are far more serious
and require regular tablets
and exercise.
so you take him to the park every day
and some people look at the lump on his side
and then they look at you as if you're a monster.
some even say: why don't you have it put down
it's cruel!
and you say
the pet says it doesn't hurt him.
but then he starts to smell so much
even your friends start commenting
and stop coming around so often
and he has a stroke
and the vet says he thinks it's
time
so you give him his last can of dog food
noticing for the first time
that it's kangaroo meat
and he refuses to eat

no matter how much you cajole.
so you take him to the vet
and after
in the waiting room
the vet says
with a sad face
it was painless mr. c.
and after a pause
he adds
by the way
a friend of mine
has these cute little puppies
he wants to get rid of…

a man running thru the dark of the day

a man runs silently thru the day
there is darkness in the adverbs of his action

the traffic can't hear itself think
the sky is as calm as a bank

the bank of clouds drops no rain
on the umbrellas of the poor

the man reaches his house
it is covered in the rain of his fears

inside, everything seems strangely normal
he listens to the silence of the walls

he turns on the tv and everything disappears
he too disappears and the tv

goes on talking
the volume rising
and the light

backyard peach tree sutra

i go out the back
the possums are waiting
high up in the peach tree
against the bright night sky
there is no wisdom
there is no attainment
i say to them
they come down
one of them chases the other
back to the top of the tree
and comes down again
there is no wisdom
there is no attainment whatsoever
i say to it
it comes closer
it is looking for some bread
i give it a piece of crust
it runs back up into the tree
i call the other one down
and give it a piece of crust
it sits there eating it
looking around anxiously
eating quickly

i am not the trick of the flower

i am not the trick of the flower
i am the flower
i no longer care what you think of me

i am effort and idleness
i have earned this claim
i am not the trick of the flower

i eat dirt and sun, drink the rain
i am larger than my circumference
i no longer care what you think of me

i am not what you have captured
i am beyond analysis
i am not the trick of the flower

i am not practicing to be a flower
i am the flower
i no longer care what you think of me

i am the earth and the sun
and the rain
i am not the trick
i no longer care what you think

paradise

the man is concentrating

his whole attention

on the rope

under his feet

straining

to lift himself

from the hole

he jumped into

to get the rope

the endeavour of strangers

when we got to the wharf
the boat was about to leave
everyone on board was grinning and
a great murmur rose like steam

we stepped close to the edge
and they put out their hands
as if to take us with them
but really they were pushing us away

and when we looked closely
their smiles were made of paint
their shoes were nailed to the decks

and they were moaning like cattle

soon the boat was a speck
and we went home
along the bloodwashed streets
to our hot little houses

from time to time
we heard rumours
that some had jumped overboard
or been pushed or else
they had disappeared in strange ports

then for a long time there was nothing
until one day in the killing yards

we saw a magazine article
reporting that there were only five of them left

and they had turned into wooden statues
but there were no photos
and we have never seen
or heard of them again

do you see that cloud
disappearing?
too late!

ant nest –
so large
we tiptoe by!

sitting on a hill
you let your mind go –
clouds

diary entry
december 7th –
buy new diary

amerika

although the tide will be low
you will be able to swim

does the doctor fill the candies?
does the waiter examine the patients?
does the receptionist dictate the letters?
does the chairman deliver the mail?

the doctor gave danny an injection
danny wanted to feel better

he read the newspaper
then he watched television.
we looked in all the stores
then we did some sightseeing

they sent us a picture
we wanted to recognize them when we met

if you need money
you go to the bank.
if you are sick
you call a doctor.
if you want a good table
you have to reserve one.
if you go to college
you get a good education.

i finished college
then i worked in an office for two years.

those people look like they have a lot of money.

it is time you bought a new car
it is time sue got married.

yes, you can get medicine at the drug store.

if i had a lot of money
i would buy an island.
if you left your jobs
you would look for other jobs.

if they went to a discotheque
they would dance
if he could not have his suit cleaned
he would have to wear another suit
if he had hated medicine
he would not have taken it
i will buy you a present
if you give me some money.

not now, but she used to be beautiful when she was young
not now, but he used to have a lot of money
when he was a famous actor

he likes the kind of car
which goes faster than other cars.

since it is after three o'clock
the bank will be closed.

since he spent all his money
he could not buy a watch.

ann is less attractive than sue
sue is more attractive than ann
jean is more attractive than sue
jean is the most attractive girl.

i will go to the theatre on thursday
sue will be with me
we will not go to the nightclub after the play
all the nightclubs will be too crowded
we will go to a restaurant for dinner
i will have steak but sue will not
she will have lobster
we will be thirsty after the play
so i will get beers for us
i will go to sue's hotel with her
it will be very late and her parents will be in bed
they will not be angry with us

the computer turns itself off at night.

(NB: these lines were selected and arranged from an
American-English textbook *circa* 1960 – upper case
letters have been removed by the author)

reincarnation explained

always

remember

if

you

come

back

as

a

cockroach

it'll

only

be

for

a

couple

of

weeks

einstein, buddhism and my stiff neck

einstein didn't discover relativity
he just had a relatively good understanding of it.
does this make him a buddhist?
some people i know
and tina turner
claim to be buddhists.
i wonder what this means.
does this make me a buddhist?
like this woman i know
an ex-landlady of mine
– she was a socialist then –
i saw her in the street a while ago
telling some people
as i hurried past
i'm a buddhist now
i wanted to go back and ask her
what does that mean?
does it mean she understands what everything is about now?
she was sort of looking at these people
as if she did –
sort of smiling knowingly at them
as if she expected something from them –
congratulations or a bowl of rice
or extreme reverence or something.
one of the reasons i'm thinking about this now is
i met another buddhist in the street today.
i've only known him for a little while
but he has managed to tell me
in a roundabout way

that he is a buddhist
and in the street today.
he seemed uncomfortable about something.
he then asked me when my party was.
two days ago, i said.
oh, he stammered
i honestly forgot when it was.
was he being a buddhist then?
i didn't care all that much
if he came to my party or not
but i didn't say that of course.
instead i said, rather snidely,
as long as you didn't *dis*honestly forget!
and we both sort of laughed
tho there was a difference in our laughter.
were we being buddhists?
i've had a stiff neck for about a week now
and it's a real pain in the arse
and that *is* funny
because
after i saw this buddhist today
i went for a bit of a bushwalk
and crossing a creek
instead of concentrating
on where i was stepping
i was thinking about these buddhists
and buddhism
wondering if there's any time
when a buddhist isn't a buddhist,
and if so,
what are they then?
and are there buddhists
who are more buddhist

than other buddhists?
and do the ultimate buddhists
(if there is such a thing)
tell people they're buddhists?
and how does a person know
he or she is a buddhist?
and what are people
if they're not buddhists?
so like i say,
i was crossing this creek
wondering about these buddhists
instead of concentrating
where i was stepping
and i slipped on a rock
and fell in the creek
badly banging my hip
– nothing broken
but it's very sore
and yet
it sure took my mind off my stiff neck for a while.

bananas

i wish there was more
time to realise
less time
but there's no room for reality
how many bananas
are there in a bunch
i bet you're thinking in figures
the great maths of the cosmos
comes down to zero plus
but don't get me wrong
i'm not this enlightened
all the time
i get angry at glances
and i don't care what you say
people are talking about me
if you spend enough time alone
even the walls become articulate
meanwhile
you're walking down the street
watching the magpie family
warbling on the nature strip
and someone who believes in something
smaller than the infinite
lets the bomb of their ignorance
blow the street away

walking down the street I

walking down the street
i saw a man
looking up at the sky
i looked up at the sky
but i couldn't see anything
so i said to him:
what're you looking at, mate?
and he looked at me and said:
the sky.

walking down the street II

walking down the street
i saw a man looking up at a tree.
i looked up at the tree
but i couldn't see anything.
so i said
what're you looking at, mate?
and he looked at me and said
that bloody magpie
it just swooped me!
and he showed me a scratch on his head.
i looked at the tree again
and saw the magpie
and just as i looked at it
it flew off.
there it goes, i said.
where? the man asked
looking in the wrong direction.

this dog today then

writing a poem
letting it come
falling like a wave off a rock
i went and looked at the sea
it was big
a ship and a rainbow on the horizon
big white clouds in the sky
the surfers
sitting legless on the water
waiting for their thrill
a smashed motorbike
red and black
in the rocks
at the base of the cliff
a woman with a ponytail
large brown jumper
track pants pulled up over her brown calves
staring down at the bike
a long time
and walking back home
sky stark blue
with gold and grey clouds
people being walked by their latest in dogs
this dog walks himself home
wondering where last year's dogs go
some people say hello as they pass
at home
i light the gas fire

turn on the radio
turn it off
look in the kitchen
it's still there.

aparty

you're asked to a party
people separate in rooms
cocaine in the bedroom
dope and techno in the lounge
booze spills across the varnished floor
the food-dips are *macrobiotic*
and conversations are earnest
and in the kitchen
the chaos of cupboards
and unreadable clocks
bring some relief
till you find yourself
outside
where the trees weep fresh air
on the footpath's dreaming
of ancestral rocks
conversing with parked cars
about times when
a waterfall flowed in the park
when the place was
'full of aboriginals
a sacred site
you know
where it ends now
in that natural amphitheatre'
and you remember
someone saying this at the party
and you recalled the place

saying *yes*
remembering how it's now used for picnics
and the occasional fringe theatre show
and off to the left
there's a smelly little creek
trickling into the pond
where not even lilies will grow
and lotus
are as far away as the stars

as we speak the ground is moving

in the morning the bedroom
floor is moving you put out
a hand to steady and the wall
is moving you slide into the
kitchen and note the moving
garden through the moving
window the birds in the trees
and the ants on the walls are
moving the trees and the fence
are moving the sky is moving
or is it the clouds

the room is blue glass
a red framed window or painting
the sky and trees fly
in the wind like birds or aeroplanes
there are people in the street
dressed in purple and green
you splash yellow and red
across the room and up the blue walls
the sound of laughter or crying
is coming from the garden
somewhere near the fake sandstone wall
covered in ivy or is it morning glory
that the car smashed into last night
sending a spray of fire into the trees
you can see where they are scorched
or else it is the shadows

as we speak the ground is moving
this is a new page
tonight the sun is weeping flame
the apples are low with worms
when the rats rise from the dump
their eyes shine like wet leaves
so much for your chatter old man
eat your rice and bang your drum
even the mosquitoes avoid you
and the dog can smell your breath
the centre of the universe is a tic on a twig
come closer to the fire light
the barren hill
is breathing still

another sunday arvo

sharon was playing her guitar
and singing her songs
when marion came in the back door.
she was drunk and angry
and she told us
she'd just had a fight with benny.
she sat down and listened to sharon
who was singing a song called
your mechanical devices
and after a few minutes
she suddenly stood up and shouted:
i'll give you your mechanical fucken devices!
with which she started undoing her false leg.
it was a warm day
the window was open
we were three floors up
and when marion had her leg off
she raised it above her head
hopped across the room
and threw it out the window.
she then sat down
and put her face in her hands
and started to cry.
sharon had stopped singing
and was staring open mouthed at her.
i went over and put my arm around marion
and told her that sharon wasn't singing that song about her.
she stopped crying then
and i went and looked out the window.

marion said:
i hope it didn't hit anyone!
and we all laughed.
the leg was lying on the pavement
so I went down and got it
and brought it back up.
marion took it from me
and put it on again
but when she stood on it
it seemed to be broken.
she didn't seem to fazed about this
so we sat around
and had a smoke
and talked
and listened to sharon
playing her guitar and singing
until benny came over
and we helped marion down the stairs
and into the car
and they drove away.

dreaming of robert de niro

robert de niro and i are in a café
he's showing me how to punch holes in the wall
and i'm doing okay –
we've already punched a few holes in the wall.
then there are five other men
in the dark light
talking to him
but looking at me
from under their hats.
i've got my silver pistol out
wrapped in the silk handkerchief in my lap
and one of the men with the hats
points his gun at me
and fires
but i beat him to the draw
shooting him dead
and the other one
against the wall
i shoot him too
before he can fire.
the other men call a halt to things then
they say i'm okay
and robert de niro says
he told them i was okay
and they say, yair well
we just had to find out for ourselves.
then they're gone
and robert de niro and i
punch a few more holes in the wall

it

it's not money
it's not food
it's not exercise
it's not music
it's not drugs
it's not the sea
it's not the sky
it's not the trees
it's not the little cat
waiting at the gate
    talking to you
     when you get home
      pushing its battle-scarred head
      into your stroking hand
it's not the girl who became a woman
      with her brown eyes flashing
      at you with their light
and it's not your grandmother
      flirting with you in hospital
      two weeks before she died
it's not the surfboard rider
      lost in her wave
it's not the laughter of friends
it's not hate
it's not love
it's not suicide
in any of its forms
it's not death or birth

or rebirth
it's not krishnamurti or zen
or animism or hinduism
or the tao te ching or the bible
or uluru
it's not culture
it's not art
it's not you
and it's not me
and it's not the planet
or the cosmos
or the turtles
or kangaroos' eyes
or the elephant's back
or horses' legs
it's not house or home
it's not land or mountain
it's not lake or river
or tadpole or trout
it's not a blade of grass
or a grain of sand
it's not a spider spinning its web
for the fiftieth time
it's not meat and it's not
vegetables or fruit
it's not miso or sugar or the
phone ringing or the rent
being due or the sun or
the wind or the rain or sex or
the flowers -

but it's pretty close…

beyond beyond

you stay here and soon
i hope you're agitated enough

the door is ajar
artistically speaking he said

if you don't drink the beer it goes flat
and other homilies like flies

seek the refuse
like all the dead narratives

alas horatio you will go on
like bored police sailors adolescents

high as a dog whistle
in order to breathe you keep your mouth shut

in this large machine the tilt light
it never rains

still the echelon blind
roll out these tired carpets

the centrifugal is centripetal
mirrors like butterfly wings

paradise 1 2 3

1.

when someone is in a hole
people come to the edge
and yell:
hey!
get out of that hole

2.

when someone is in a hole
and people come to the edge
and yell down:
hey! get out of that hole!
they don't get to close
in case they fall in too

3.

when someone is in a hole
and people come to the edge
and yell
hey! get out of that hole!
and the person asks for some rope
they throw down a length
and walk away
shaking their heads

wolves

we take her dog to the beach
to bathe its infected ear
and when she starts complaining
about her boyfriend again
i look away.
look, i say,
pointing at her dog
he's found a friend!
a labrador
is licking her dog's ear.
look at that! i say.
yes, she nods,
they've got a natural antiseptic in their saliva.
the wolves used to do it.
used to? i say.
oh, well, yes, she says.
i suppose they still do
the ones who're left.
i hear their numbers are increasing, i say.
coming back, in germany and places.
wolves? she says.
yes, wolves.
that's good, i like wolves.
me too, i say,
and we look at the dogs –
and they're looking at us.

asylum

	i want to write a political poem about how
	the asylum seekers are being treated like the
aborigines	were treated up until the 1960s (and even
	now in some places) and how the people who
	are imprisoning
asylum seekers	for up to 3 years are the descendants of the
	people who were either
immigrants	or convicts or people who invaded in boats
	and took over and how they seem to be
	afraid these asylum seekers and anyone else
	who comes here who looks different will
	take over the way their
ancestors	did and how peaceful this old country has
	always been until these men have come into
power	are so scared they are scaring our neighbours
	and all the lessons of 1914 and 1939 will
	have to be gone through again but i'm too
	angry to write anything but this blank piece
	of prose without any kind of meaningful
	ending except to say there is no ending to
	anything because we are not the universe
	although we are it
	too

ontos farm

everything still and flying
kookaburras and parrots
the constellations
the song of the castanet frogs
like aborigines chanting
harmonies of the ground
singing the sky
relentless and going for it
then stopping
to listen
just one going on like a clap stick
until it too stops
everything still
listening to itself
time and eternity
earth and sky
wallabies kissing in a twilight field
holding straws in their little hands
ears revolving
all this and the joey
and the young shoots of clover
they love so much

yarra yarra (ever flowing river)

I

REELAHCOHGARRA	the land where the sun rises
GULAWA	the place of my heart
BULAM	my native home, my native country
LOWRA	a beautiful place, place of plenty
YANCO	the sound of running water
KOORAEGULLA	good morning brother
BUMBALDRY	the sound made when men and women jump into the water
BODALLA	to toss a child up and down in the arms
QUINDALLUP	a happy place
MURRUNGUNDIE	nose and eyes at play
YAMBLE	laughing playing joking
WEJA	to love
YONGERLOCELKUCUP	a plain where the kangaroos dance
CULKINEWARINEBINELUP	a place where palms grow profusely
YEOLANGS	a black cockatoo with a red tail
FERRITCARTUP	plenty of silver wattle trees
BOMBALA	meeting of the waters
WITGWERI	wind whistling through the sheoaks
GERINGONG	fear – the place where aborigines first saw the sails of Cook's "Endeavour" and expressed their fear
MUKINTUNDUNRUP	the moon rising over the hills

BEPERA   place where a woman ran away
                                when the moon rose

GIRILAMBONE   place where a star fell

II

ULMURRA   a bend in the river
CURROON   fog on top of a mountain
KOOLANJIN   forked sticks in the ground
QUEERBRI   fish swim quick
MUGIMULLEN   can't go to sleep
TAMALEE   lie down on your belly
ONNUA   white man with gun
TEERAWAH   an angry rainbow
TOMINGLEY   look out! there's a death adder!
ADURLU   a white man's camp
BOOREBUCK   a prepared place where initia-
                                tion ceremonies are held, and
                                therefore a sacred place

BABAWALTHI   bad water
BARRINGUM   fish die in the water
BOONBOOLONG   place of the evil one, a spirit who
                                has the ability to turn himself into
                                various forms

BOORLAHBOORLOO   a place where grass does not
                                grow; never green

TARRANA   a place where a woman was
                                ravaged

BUCKAWACKAH   to crawl on hands and knees
BULLIGEMA   troopers dispersing aborigines
BUMBALDRY   sound made when men and
                                women jump into the water

QUIDONG   the place of the echo

TEERAWAH	an angry rainbow
GILLAMAGONG	house of the big white man
BOOKA BOOKA	many bad smells
COWABBIE	name given to cows when first seen
WIRRABILLA	water with teeth in it
WANDANANDONG	spirits who persecute the souls of the dead in an underworld
CUBTAHPOOLIMAN	an aboriginal policeman
DOOLANGHOOTERGHU	a man becoming agitated when crossing a bog, feeling his way with a stick, and suddenly finding that it is disappearing in the soft mud
DULCOONGHI	a place of sickness
MUGIMULLEN	can't go to sleep
ONNUA	white man with gun
COONDOO	a death adder
GANGALOOK	echo
COMBO	a terror for women
CODOBINE	where a man removed the heart of another
THAAHMARLKEEPENK	the name of an invisible spirit with sharp projecting elbows who drives people mad by prodding them with his elbows
BURGOONEY	ants tunnelling in sandy soil
ELLENGERAH	a man eating white pebbles
MICKELLOO	white man
TARBOONKINKILL	a white woman
BOORRAIBERRIMA	to struggle violently
BUCKAWACKAH	to crawl on hands and knees
BOGONG	place infested with fleas

WEEMOBAH	a place of permanent fire
BILLABUNG	dead reach of water
ROORCARIRULTADUANNAARAH	
	one tree on a hill
ULAH	a ripple on the water
ULMARRA	a bend in the river
AMAH	aboriginal man
JUNDAH	aboriginal woman
KOORAEGULLA	good morning brother
KOORAEGULLA	good morning brother
WAHROONGA	my home, our home

III

WAREELAHCOHGARRA	the land where the sun rises
TUGULAWA	the place of the heart
CHITTENNUP	place of the white flower
WEJA	love
YIDDAH	to recover from sickness
BOMBALA	meeting of the waters
PURPUR	a creek where there are plenty of turtles
WOONINGCANNING	where wild ducks flock and play together
WAROOKA	a parrot with beautiful feathers
AKMA	fresh water
BINTAMILING	many red flowers
MURRUNGUNDIE	nose and eyes at play
MANGOPLAH	people singing
QUINDALUP	a happy place
ANEMBO	peaceful, quiet place
ULAH	a ripple on the water

WACKNARUNGYUKA   tree of curiosity
YARRA YARRA   ever flowing river

[Note: This poem was created from a selection of aboriginal place names and their meanings taken from *Aboriginal Place Names*, by A.W. Reed. Published by A. H. & A.W. Reed Pty. Ltd. 1967]

bar-b-q in blue

for Sue

i'm in Fitzroy
and my sister's just left the police force
picks me up
            for dinner
but, oh
    i won't mind
going to a bar-b-q
                    they've organized
for her farewell?
no…!
the little plastic bag in my coat pocket
takes on more significance
and my appearance

fourteen cops in the lounge room log fire
i keep my coat on
i'm hot
i'm quiet
i'm strange
but i'm my sister's brother okay?
av a beer, grant
                the sergeant sez
i drink lots
the cops have clean shirts
they talk about
work

one of them has too much
                     after-shave
the young girls look at me quickly
mary the mother
serves steaks, chops, sausages, patties,
       coleslaw, potato-salad, tomato sauce
                     knives and forks
husband stan
        shakes my hand
the eyes of mother mary say
                 but you look so thin

my sister checks her perfunctory clock
we leave
      with goodbyes
             all round
             heh heh

nice people eh?
my sister in her car
yair... sure...

the edge of the forest

when they reached the edge of the forest they stopped and
waited listening for some time but there was no sound and so
they continued waiting they could neither go forward nor back
and eventually they were unsure if they had been coming out
of the forest or going into it they tried to recall what they had
been doing or what they had learned but it all seemed too long
ago and so they decided they just had to keep waiting and
listening unsure what they would do even if they did remember
even if they did hear something even if something did happen
even if something had happened

on her loud yellow walkman

on the packed bus
a voice from the front
can someone give me a seat please
i've only got one leg
and with much shuffling and movement
he gets his seat
a young man
barely twenty
and everyone becomes gravely silent
but for the girl
singing along with madonna
on her loud yellow walkman

rented house trilogy

where birds fly like sparks across the sky

this day of high winds
where birds fly like sparks across the sky
i go out
and meet old next-door joe
coming at me with
your trees!
i have to sweep my path
three times a day!
what are you going to do?
you have to
chop them down!
i tell him
what to do with his
chop them down
and now
his window is wide open
and he's playing his tv
loud as he can
i get up
put the sex pistols on
volume ten
open my window
sit down
and relax

this hot night

this hot night
it's
lighter and cooler
outside
i go out
look at the sky
the stars
the light
from the moon
the streetlights
coming over the roofs
the sound of men's voices
a car
idling
then
moving away
old joe's light
is still on
tho it's late.
today
i got the knockback
from the bank
for the loan
writers are not
a good risk
i suppose
i'll have to leave here now
moving again
searching for another bargain haven
in the cluster of streets
i breathe deep and

hard
the huge poplar by the front gate
is still
its little green leaves turned
up to the stars
oh well
at least
i no longer
need decide
whether to try and buy this dump
now
i walk around the back
touch my old friend
the big ghost gum
it says nothing
it says everything
we breathe
deep into the night

terra nullius

the day of the auction
there were lots of people
coming through my house
lyn and me
sat in the kitchen
talking and smoking and
drinking tea
trying to ignore them
until the auctioneer began
and we went out the front
to watch
20 minutes later

it was sold
for $80,500
to a man from box hill
bought it for his son
to renovate
when i went inside
ten minutes later
they were all there
the vendor
the father and his son
and the agent
sitting in my chair
at my desk
preparing the documents
with my lamp on
i asked them then
if they were going to
continue renting it to me
no, i'm sorry, the father said
i hope it's not an inconvenience
of course it's an inconvenience
i said
i almost shouted
and they, all four of them
jumped
so you're a writer
the father said
my brother-in-law's a writer
he writes speeches
for the prime minister
i didn't say anything
i kept looking at the agent
at my desk
sitting in the light of my lamp

a short history of the future

in uncertain glass you
wake and wake to
the history tapes
in nests of space

you wake and wake
to eyes of loss and longing
in nests of space
strange in their appearance

these eyes of loss and longing
you can't concede
how strange is their appearance
in spite of their commotion

you can't concede
as long as the stars
in spite of the commotion
rise above the morning

as long as the stars
in the singing space of scars
rise above the morning
immense as atoms

in the singing space of scars
your mind sails on
immense as atoms
in the illusion of such stillness

your mind sails on
each moment stacked
in the illusion of such stillness
like ancestral graveyards

each moment stacked
like books of light
or ancestral graveyards
true to spacetime

like books of light
the science of feeling
is true to spacetime
or scattered matter

this science of feeling
the history tapes
or scattered matter
in uncertain glass you

the colour of black light

hot summer monday
i've got eleven dollars till friday
i go down the street
the dogs are crapping in the park
the birds are singing in the trees
the clouds are high and bright and white
people tearing around in their cars
looking for parking
i go to a second-hand haunt
    find a box of books
    sort out fifteen paperbacks –
    hesse faulkner koestler etc.
    and one turgenev i haven't read
    they come to $12.60 but
    the woman lets me have them for eleven
i walk into town
the sun is eating the pavement
i'm glad i have my hat
i go to nick's bookshop with the books
he gives me $34
and i keep the turgenev

we talk a while
me and nick and simon
about writing and drugs and booze
and it comes around to bukowski
nick says it's all very well to
get blind drunk
write two great poems

shit in your landlady's letterbox
go out and fuck two whores
go home and write another great poem
get drunk again
get an abusive phone call from your publisher
write a poem about it
fuck your landlady
write a poem about how she shit in your letterbox
etc etc
but he doesn't talk about the pain
all the spewing and the blood and the
passing out in strangers' gardens…
well, he does, actually, i say
tho he once said
no-one wants to hear about the pain
they just want to laugh

i get a bus back to the junction
they let you spend up to one thousand dollars
the woman behind me says
…and the payments are only ten dollars a week
that's good her friend says
yes isn't it! the first woman says
i get off the bus
buy some food envelopes stamps and
head home
the wind is up
it's still hot but
there's a chill in the air
very subtle
it's like a chilled heat
i get home
the boys are yelling in the park

there's a christmas card from my publisher
and a cheque from a newspaper for $39
for a poem they published
i go inside
open all the windows
and lie on the floor

i make some dinner
watch a doco on SBS on matisse
who brought everything down
to pure form and colour
he said
you have to see everything
as if for the first time
you have to see things
like a child
you must not lose that
i read a newspaper
i found in the post office
then i turn out all the lights
and look at the night
breathing in the night air
it's dark and yet light and
i remember something else about matisse
how someone said he
used the colour black
as light
the woman next door has a visitor
some guy keeps coming around
she half pretends she's pleased to see him
they sort of kiss at the door
i watch a game of soccer on tv
leeds v tottenham

one-all but
leeds should have won
i sit and think about nothing
have some dandelion coffee
read some turgenev
a dog barks somewhere
the man in number 6
slams his door
i look out the window again
i notice the trees are waving
i imagine they're waving at me
waving their big green hands at me in the moonlight
then i wonder
if they are waving at me
are they waving hello
or goodbye
and if so
who's going anywhere anyway

kitchen roof –
leaking
into cooking pots

summer rain
in the overgrown garden –
head of the buddha

loud rain –
when it stops
someone is shouting

tied to the railing
above the old ford centre –
aboriginal flag

you-poem

you've been talking
about yourself again
your ears are ringing

letting your hook run
downriver to your memory
casting no shadows

death is busy in foreign lands
the slate is clean red this year

your humanity is in the lounge room
like a comfortable chair

you sit in it
when guests arrive

they sit on the floor
hoping something funny will occur

the progress of inane sense

the child falls backwards
hands in the air
crying like a window on fire
breaking the field in squares
the auctioneer adjusts his blinkers
he looks like a dragonfly
the drought will pass, he says
as long as the enemy dies

in the shelter
the wind turns on itself
and thousands of fairies with burning wings
cover the floor with their screaming

meanwhile your young tongue is a balloon
the earth hisses horizons of endlessness
the caves, it says, the caves
and leave all your promises

the sky is alive with an emptiness
and each breath tastes like iron
ahead the broken mountains
lift like black smashed teeth
or vultures' wings
with the sun on their tips
and rising

pleasure comes again (like

the question of existence
how many lives do you want
the payments become increasingly sage-like
is this the test of your detachment
not to run away (again
there is no how to but
the old peach tree is flowering again
the years of nostalgia are gathering
for the final defeat
of your frame
are you going to stand there till you drop
you know there are castles to be built
you see the approaching horizon
blue and black and elusive
the sky in your mind opening
the pain your buried stone

free bison with the net up

after Robert Frost who said:
Writing free verse is like
playing tennis with the net down.

police used a helicopter
and a dozen cars to corral
a wayward herd
of bison roaming
through an upmarket
suburb of baltimore
on tuesday. the nine
animals disrupted traffic
and alarmed residents
before they were herded
onto a tennis court.
the bison were loose
in pikesville, a gated community
in the u.s. east coast state of maryland.
police used lounge chairs
beside the tennis court
as shields and formed
a human chain. one animal
leapt the net
as it tried to evade capture. once
cornered, the animals were returned
to the farm from where they came.
the owner told the *new york times*
the beasts
would be slaughtered for mince

you have control now

you have control now
well done. lock the doors
don't even let the ants in
you know they don't love you
the television doesn't love you
you can see what's wrong
from your closed window
you can shake your poetic head at
how silly it all is
you can watch the sky and marvel
but you are not a part
of it any more you are in your
spaceship and the world is a book
and soon you will be so alone no-one
will be speaking your language no-one will
see you no-one not even you will have
any idea of you and whatever remains
will know that this is what you always
wanted

tobin bronze

he's probably dead now
but in 1967
i was a student
at caulfield
caulfield cup day
there to back him mainly
the big chestnut
with the golden mane –
he was six-to-one
with 59 kilos.
all the smarties
reckoned he couldn't carry it
the one and a half miles
against those other champions
some with 9 or 10 kilos less.
i had a few small wins in the earlier races
so i put $30, two weeks' rent
on the nose
and went up half an hour early
to get a seat in the stand
overlooking the winning post
watching the big crowd
filling the gaps
the rising noise
and the colours
down on the grass
and then the horses
starting to parade
in the saddling enclosure.

you could pick him
before his number went on
he stood out
and not just for his size.
my heart was beginning to bang in my chest
and not just because of the money
taking in every second of the parade –
the hoops in their silks
swinging up
into their saddles
adjusting their straps
listening to the last-minute instructions.
and big tobin
leading them out
onto the track
in front of the stand
packed now
to the rafters –
stopping there tho
in the gate
so all the others had to wait
so everything and everyone
had to wait
standing there
no matter how much the jockey urged
standing and turning his head
to look at the crowd
all waiting
just for him
to lift his head like that
to look at them like that
like some kind of proclamation
lifting his tail like that

his golden tail
to let drop
the golden bricks of his bowels
on the hallowed turf
for all those following
to walk through.
it was the way he did it
got me most of all
before dropping his tail again
and walking onto the course
and cantering off
around towards the start.
i gave up my seat in the stand
ran down the six flights of stairs
and had the rest of my money
another $30
on the nose
getting 13-to-2 now.
and by the time i got back
i could hardly get into the stand
let alone a seat or standing room.
so i climbed the wall by the stairs
and hung from the rafters
like some kind of monkey
where i could see everything clearly
alternating arms
to ease the strain
which i forgot when the race began.
i couldn't hear the broadcast
for the noise of the crowd
but it didn't matter
i could see big tobin
second or third last

all
the
way
around
in the field of twenty-four
not starting his move
till well before the top turn
then coming on
ranging wide around them
so when they turned for home
two furlongs out
and they fanned
eight or nine wide across the track
he was out in no-man's land
he was mowing them down
i was yelling my heart out
leaping about like a lunatic
hanging from my arms
as he gobbled them up
storming home
down the middle of the track
the most beautiful animal you could see
and it wasn't just the money
it was the way he did it
streaking away
winning by two lengths or more
going away on the line.
i was shaking like a bastard
as i dropped to my feet in the crowd
running down the stairs
my legs like jelly
repeating
over and over

as i went:
you fucking beauty!
you fucking beauty!
heading for the bookie's payout line
changing with every step
a man
into a gambler!

the philosophy of brakes

in the middle of this circle
something like a clock
with the threat of tomorrow
coming like a train with no driver
or no brakes
this is what we hold on to
the philosophy of brakes
or the philosophy of drivers
meanwhile you can't sleep
you have lost control of your abandonment
the dreams you ordered have not arrived again
your body looks at you like a child or a dog
you ignore it or worse you
give it something to shut it up
and the circle moves a little
closer

beach balls

daylight glory
on a sudden beach

how pacific you seem
strolling like water
the waves
eating your toes

far-off arguments
stumble on each other
like beach balls
as if horizons can be trusted

the sea saves you
drowning in sand

zone

now the burgeoning
as we move along the glorious trench
safe from the horizon of anxieties

soon balloons
will signal escape
or attack

the material in your pocket
is not an illusion
but the pocket is

so many avenues in the sky
if you think about it
there's no stopping

soon another soon
everyone is looking correctly
in the wrong direction
or vice versa

essay on the determinate and language

after Jaques Derrida

to say what you mean when
you're not sure what you (mean
when everything sounds so (trite
how beautiful is an egg and (why
why is such an ugliness (like how
the scientists have so much to answer for
the reason everything is
presumed to be explicit (like
the radiation of the field produces the electrode
but what produces the radiation (energy
o
the universe might be curved but what's beyond
the curve etcetera the answer is what a dead branch
falling on a grassy bank in the spring sunshine by a
lake where ducks paddle after insects and carp and
two people lie together
is

phantom pains

the phantom pains
in your missing legs
grow each day
you reflect
the unshaven face
of your persona
you take the cutthroat razor
your father left you
sharpen it on the strop
he once threatened
to belt you with
for your own good
you gaze out the window
of your flat
at the windows
of other flats
you hear the midday show
on the woman next door's tv
you smell boiled cabbage and fried liver
coming from the old man's kitchen
across the hall
you hear the scream
of a child somewhere
and a bird flies past your window
just at the moment you looked there
　　　a blackbird you're sure
you recall its song
you once listened to
in your mother's garden

you remember the shrubs and the fruit trees
how you fell out of the pear tree
and broke your arm
how your mother fussed over you
how you didn't have to go to school for a week
how you played wounded soldiers with yourself
in the backyard
and listened through the fence like a spy
to the man and woman next door
shouting at each other

you look out the window again
hoping to see another bird

the sky in your brain now

words like birds singing
you land them on the white grass
their black forms dance at the worms of your grace
the breeze moves pinkly through the trees
the land is otherwise still in thought
as if something is imminent or
has occurred something
so large that it will not
be noticed until it is gone

the light embraces
even the shadows now
the predators are all in cages
or jars but what are those
spectral movements those
formless twists in the dark air
that spike the manicured verges

of course you're an ideal prisoner
in the window of dreams
there are no bars and the guards
let you play with their guns
you paint them
red
blue or yellow
and lay them down
to dry in the sun and the breeze
blows
their metallic odour
across the flowers of your brain

blue cage

when you think even the walls
have it in for you
you see everyone grasping the air
like they're on fire

when the pain of missing of
avoiding not avoiding being
caught in the capsule like
a cage in the gullet of a giant

when it's too early in the morning
and your thoughts your history
shakes you awake
like a baby

when all this and more like
how words are never quite enough
when you start to think that suicide
is an easy way to sleep

when you're too immersed to
see like a wombat or a beetle
when all this and all this
won't stop suddenly

you hear the sigh of rain on the roof
like the whisper of a mother saying
it's all right, darling, everything
is all right

and slowly slowly
you feel yourself smiling
and you begin to feel true sleep
calling like a lover and the walls
no longer exist

two black chairs

from up here
in this side room at the wedding reception
i'm looking down
through a window
across the street below
into a restaurant window
framed in fairy lights
dancing in the dark delight of night
below a neon *seafood and wine* sign and
inside on the wall above a fireplace
there is a picture of elvis before his dissipation
looking over white tables and a couple
talking, their heads close and next
door a shop window is lit up but empty
empty but for two black chairs
lit up in the lit up empty shop window
two black chairs
half facing each other
as if they are talking
in the stark light of the bare shop light
while up here i am alone and
in the next room through the partition
the wedding party dances and laughs to imitation salsa
and in the seafood and wine restaurant below
framed in dancing fairy lights the waitress
sets cutlery on the white clothed tables
and the couple with their heads close are
looked over by elvis before his dissipation
and next door the two black chairs regard each other

in the harsh light of the empty shop window
while up here in this room
there is a white rose and a black purse
on the table by the door
and through the partition
the wedding party dances and laughs
in the dimmed light to imitation salsa
and i sit alone like the two black chairs
thinking of elvis before his dissipation
and the waitress in the wine bar
overhears the couple by the fireplace
talking of marriage and she thinks
of her husband at home with their child
and her purse she left in the kitchen with the rent
in it and next door in the empty light of the empty
shop window the empty black chairs are afraid
to move in the empty shop sharp light
while up here someone laughs and dances
into the room to retrieve her purse she
smiles at me and i wonder if we should marry
while across the street in the restaurant below
the waitress has disappeared and the couple
are kissing below elvis before his dissipation
and the chairs in the empty shop window have
moved closer and the light is dimmer while
up here i move out of the empty room and
into the thrall of the laughter and salsa dancing
almost everyone is dancing almost everyone is
laughing and talking and around the room
almost all the chairs are empty almost all
the lights are dimmed and almost everyone
is dancing and laughing even the woman with the black
purse she is dancing by herself and she

gestures to me and i join her and she tells me her name
and we are across the street in the restaurant
sitting at the white table watched over by elvis before his
dissipation poor elvis stuck on the wall in his youth and
we are surrounded by fairy lights dancing in the dark
night's delight and the waitress is taking our order
and we are telling her of our marriage plans and she
says it is so romantic and she lights our candle and i look
around at the empty tables and chairs and the empty fireplace
and i wonder where everyone is and as if she can read my
thoughts the waitress says they are all next door can't i hear
them talking and laughing because there is an art exhibition
opening there and a poet is reading a famous poet is opening
the show and everyone is laughing and absorbed in his words
and yet wondering why he is holding a white rose and why
there are two empty black chairs on the stage with him facing
towards the shop window and the dark street and why is
there a black purse on one of them and why does he keep
mentioning elvis before his dissipation and fairy lights and
weddings and what is all this about people dancing and
laughing in the next room almost everyone is wondering this
almost everyone is unsure just what is real and what is his
invention almost everyone is wondering even he is wondering
only the two chairs the two black chairs are not they are not
wondering they are half facing each other in the stark light the
stark light of the empty shop window looking out of the empty
shop window out onto the empty street lit by the streetlights lit
by the lonely dim streetlights stretching their
dim light and dimly light the street
never fail to dimly light the street
never fail
to dimly light the street

white butterflies
flitting through the rose bushes
while they can

summer sunset
alone on the beach –
driftwood

waves at night –
the moon
through clouds

sitting by the creek
a thousand years pass
sitting by the creek